NATURE'S LESSONS

PATRICIA LEE APPELT

God's Blessings
Patricia Appelt

America Star Books

Softcover 9781629071923
PUBLISHED BY AMERICA STAR BOOKS, LLLP
www.americastarbooks.com

Printed in the United States of America

Dedication

When my first book HORIZONS was published and purchased by some of my colleagues at Clifton Springs Hospital & Clinic, I received a telephone call from Dr. Les Moore; the director of the Spa. He specifically requested permission to include some of my poetry in his project of compiling local poetry. After Dr. Moore was granted his request, he explained to me his reason for including my poetry; that my poetry is so natural and about nature!

Dr. Moore:
I dedicate NATURE'S LESSONS to you for your subtle way of encouraging me to continue writing and to share my appreciation of nature.
Thank you Dr. Moore for being a catalyst!
Thank you Dr. Moore for your request from over five years ago!
Thank you Dr. Moore for our friendship as colleagues!
Enjoy sharing our friendship in the reading of NATURE'S LESSONS!

God's blessings, Patricia

CHAPTER 1

Nature

In the beginning God created the heaven and the earth.

Genesis 1:1

illustration by Susan LaSpagnoletta

What is Nature?

Finally brethren, whatsoever things are true, whatsoever things are honest, whatsoever things are just, whatsoever things are pure, whatsoever things are lovely, whatsoever things are of good report, if there be any virtue, and if there be any praise, think on these things. Philippians 4:8

The Apostle Paul writes a letter of advise to the bishops and deacons within the church of Philippi. He reminds them to think on that which is of virtue and worthy of praise.

I think of nature as worthy of virtue and of praise! Nature has the word true in it! God's creation of nature is true, There is no pretending! There are no false pretenses!

As a Christian created by the same God who created the heaven and the earth, I need to live; thinking on those things that are true; not needing to pretend or live my Christian life on false pretenses.

Nature also has words in it that are in a Christian's vocabulary: neat, turn, tune, and near. These few words are tucked in hymns such as
Nearer My God to Thee, Turn Your Eyes Upon Jesus, and Whisper A Prayer.

What is in nature should also be evident in our Christian nature.

...and he shall be like a tree planted by the rivers of water, that bringeth forth fruit in his season, his leaf also shall not wither; and whatsoever he doeth shall prosper.

Psalm 1: 3

The love for nature is expressed by the Psalmist and King David. He expresses the blessedness of man created to be a part of nature. We may be created as healthy as a tree planted by the rivers of water.

God gives the blessings upon the creation of our human bodies.

God alone gives the blessings upon the creation of our Christian bodies.

Our physical health depends on God's choices; what He allows.

Our Christian health depends on our choices: attitude and application.

As a child I recall the trees planted by the pond, bringing fruit, leaves clinging to the branches all because of creeks, streams, and the pond storing water for nourishment.

As an adult I recall the names of trees and am more conscious of the sources of water and recognize clubs and organizations that attempt to preserve the sources of nourishment for nature's plants.

If the Psalmist David were to live in our day; just imagine him using a laptop while tending his sheep...the words flowing rapidly across the screen. The message would not change though. Even though there are new ways to store nourishment for plants: Rapid Grow, green-houses, harvest machinery, and even grocery stores would be new vocabulary words for David, but his message would still include: blessedness, planting, creation, and God's choices in daily creation.

I pray that we will continue to recognize the blessings within God's daily creations and be recognized by our names, our Christian nature, and most of all; our healthy attitude, approach, and application of allowing God's continual blessings to help us plant, bring forth fruit, and nourish lives.

And they said one to another, Go to, let us make brick and burn them thoroughly. And they had brick for stones, and slime they had for mortar.

Genesis 11: 3

We are familiar with God's creative powers recorded by Moses in the book of Genesis. There are many construction zones: heaven and earth, creatures, man, Noah's Ark, and the Tower of Babel (which is the construction zone recorded here in Genesis 11:3).

We are familiar with the impact of a finished building; from the environment to the people afffected. For Moses the recording of this awesome tower did not include the mention of blueprints, meeting proper codes, or a list of tools including a jack-hammer! It could easily include the observation and following the example of the construction of an ant hill, or a beaver's dam, a bee hive, or a bird's nest.

As a child, I remember the finished construction zones made by our family; forts(made from wood and snow!), cabin in the woods (painted pink to keep hunters away!), the milk house (replacing milk cans with milk tanks!), and a tree house(remain standing for years). Natural resources were a major factor!

As an adult I learned from my parents' construction zone of their new home of stone, of solar energy, and created by their own hands in Portal, Arizona where progress reports, updates, and even vacations allowed for valuable lessons that have been carried down through the beginning of creation and taught by God daily:

* No matter the amount of planning, what matters is the cooperation!
* Whatever material is used, depends on the condition!
* Preparation is crucial as well as the actual construction!
* No matter the main purpose, what matters is the circumstances!
* God's planning, material, preparation and purpose in our Christian lives depends on our cooperation, conditions, allowing for construction and living within our circumstances.

CHAPTER 2

Mother Nature

Or speak to the earth, and it shall teach thee and the fowls of the air, and they shall tell thee.

Job 12:8

illustration by Susan LaSpagnoletta

Pastures

Know ye that the Lord...He is God: it is He that hath made us, and not ourselves; we are His people, and the sheep of His pasture.

Psalm 100:3

David the writer of the Psalms also has the following titles: Shepherd, Harpist, Poet, and King. He writes in today's text about the importance of pastures. He did not write about any barbed-wire fences, or huge barns.

Instead, he wrote about the protection of the trees, bushes, rocks and most of all his role as a shepherd of his flock. We know he wrote about the coming of a great shepherd that would provide protection, nourishment, and provision for mankind.

As a child I recall the protection of trees and the barbed-wire fences made from the trees. I recall the foundations and beams of buildings made from the rocks and the trees.

As an adult I recall accepting Jesus as my Saviour, Shepherd to protect, nourish, and provide for me, all because of a young camper! I recall the foundations of salvation presented to me and the character building as I was sent out from college to become one of the sheep of my Lord...my God!

CHAPTER 3

Pelicans, Owls, and Sparrows

I am like a pelican of the wilderness, I am like an owl of the desert.
I watch and am a sparrow alone upon the house top.
                                                    Psalm 102: 6,7

Once again the shepherd David writes about the careful watch of his sheep.

He compares the watching of three birds and how he watches for God's mercy.

I remember receiving a postcard from my Grandma and Grandpa Seabury from one of their Florida visits. That is my childhood and adult memory! I did some research about the pelican and recognize that the wilderness for them is often the tall reeds along the shores of the Everglades. These reeds conceal them from predators.

Dear Christian of the wilderness:
Learn from the pelican of its' continual dependence upon nature's protective reeds. We need continual dependence of God's protective grace.

I remember on the farm a rare view of a barn owl with its watchful piercing look in our up-state NY, Prattsburg farm. I have learned as an adult about the owl of the desert from visiting my parents in Portal, Arizona. Portal is the bird "sanctuary" of Arizona!. The desert vegetation can conceal the owl from predators.

Dear Christian of the desert:
Learn from the owl of its' continual dependence upon nature's protective vegetation. We need continual dependence of God's protective guidance.

I remember in my wide range of traveling the eastern coast of the U.S.A. the view of the sparrow perched on a house top or a telephone wire with its watchful eye from so many larger creatures; predators. I also recognize them as for their means of survival due to their natural color and often staying in groups.

Dear Christian of the house top;
Learn from the sparrow of its' continual dependence upon nature's protective canopy which often includes joining others on the high wire! We need continual dependence upon God's protective provision!

CHAPTER 4

Feathers of Fowl

And God said, Let the waters bring forth abundantly the moving creatures that hath life, and fowl that may fly above the earth in the open firmament of heaven.

Genesis 1:20

In Moses first book (Genesis), we are introduced to the abundance of the fowl and their existence around water, or upon the trees. When watching the flight of a bird, one observes the following: freedom, majesty, power, beauty, elegance, and flexibility.

Often when bird watchers record their findings of fowl in flight they record their wing span, and the pattern of flight. The color of their feathers may also be a way of recognizing the name of the bird.

Many colors are contained in the wings of a fowl but certain hues stand out for the: Cardinal, Jay, Robin, Finch, Hawk, and Sparrow. You as the reader may be able to list others that are unique for where you live. As a resident of New York State (specifically the Finger Lakes Region), my partial list of birds are recognized by me because of their color, their flight pattern and nesting habits.

As an amateur bird watcher, I am intrigued by the elegance, beauty, strength, and flexibility of the fowl of the air. Are others intrigued by the elegance, beauty, strength and flexibility of our lives under the protective guidance and abundance of our God?

CHAPTER 5

Nature Trail

He maketh me to lie down in green pastures, he leadeth me beside the still waters.

Psalm 23: 2

illustration by Susan LaSpagnoletta

CHAPTER 6

Skies and Streams

Then the Lord answered Job out of the whirlwind, and said,...canst thou lift up thy voice to the clouds, that abundance of waters may cover thee?

Job 38: 1 & 34

Job, was from the land of Uz; perfect and upright, one that feared God and eschewed evil (Job 1:1). He had his sincerity tested and is provoked by Eliphas (the Temanite) in Job 4 and challenged by God (Job 38).

We may have been told that we have the patience of Job. The patience of Job is our lesson today on how to meet God's challenge to patiently wait for the power of the skies and the streams.

While working at The Salvation Army, Long Point Camp on Seneca Lake, in New York during the summers of the early 1970's, I learned many lesssons from the skies and the streams. Just as Job had his sincerity tested by Eliphas and God, so I had my sincerity tested by the staff and campers at Long Point. I was challenged by God to follow him back at Fredonia, NY University each academic year. What ways could I lift up my voice to the clouds? How could I accept God's abundance around me? Would I allow Him to prepare me for His plan?

God inspired me to start a journal with entries such as; I Wonder (this was the first song I wrote). I literally lifted my voice to the clouds and let God's abundance of water cover me as I walked the campus of Fredonia University in a gentle rain:

As I look up into the sky, I watch the clouds roll by (repeat).
I begin to wonder who, wonder what, wonder when, wonder why about my life. Then I look up into the sky and smile at God who has helped my life go by.

The journal entries in the 1970's continued like a flowing stream; as the early morning light showing through the counsellor's cabin window at Long Point Camp near Penn Yan, NY. became the catylst for another song: Streams

Streams of light show through the half closed curtains of my life showing me the radiance of God's face.
Streams of trickling water run down the window pane nourishing me of the thought that God's life is flowing by.
As life goes flowing gently by the hearts of many men melt right down at the knowledge of Jesus Christ.
Streams of joy and happiness overflow within my soul Ever since I met the Saviour, He has made me whole.

Today, in 2013, I lift these same songs to God in thanks for His awesome powerful lessons found in His creation of nature.

CHAPTER 7

The First Map

And the Lord God planted a garden eastward in Eden; and there He put the man whom He had formed.

Genesis 2:8

Do you recall being a part of planning a vegetable garden map?

Do you remember studying maps in Geography?

Creating a Natural Resource Map was my favorite to study and to recreate. Today the fascination is carried over in my postcard collection of every U.S.A. state map with natural resources and other fascinating facts printed on the postcards.

Moses was descriptive about the Garden of Eden and if he had the tools of today to illustrate, he would include the natural resources of the four major rivers in the Garden of Eden. Even the names were significant:

The name of the first is Pison; that is it which compasseth the whole land of Havilah, where there is gold.

Genesis 2:11

Gold and other minerals were of value for ornaments, money treasures. We continue to find gold listed as a valuable natural resource. Are we preparing to walk heaven's streets of gold?

And the name of the second river is Gihon; the same is it that compasseth the whole land of Ethiopia.

Genesis 2:13

Gihon is an intermittent spring of value for water, nourishment, survival. We continue to find water listed as a valuable natural resource. Do we allow the quenching of our spiritual thirst?

And the name of the third river is Hiddekel; that is it which goeth toward the east of Assyria.

Genesis 2:14

Hiddekel is also known as the Tigris and excelled in the formation of irrigation systems for botanical gardens. We continue to find the value of botanical gardens that are properly irrigated. Do we show evidence of growth in beauty and grace?

And the name of the fourth river is Euphrates. Genesis 2:14

Euphrates is the largest river in West Asia with a region called
Mesopotamia containing animal life such as fallow deer (hart).
We continue to find the value of animal life for a natural resource.
Do we follow our Lord Jesus Christ (also called the Lamb of God)?

CHAPTER 8

Nature's Mirrors

As in water face answereth to face, so the heart of man to man.

Proverbs 27:19

Solomon writes how water is nature's mirror; presenting an exact mirror. According to Webster's New Dictionary a mirror is any surface capable of reflecting sufficient undifused light to form a visual image of an object placed in front of it.

Standing in front of a puddle of water, nestled in the rut of a narrow country lane, is a creature. The the fowl or beast stands facing its own reflection, sipping and enjoying nourishment.

Oh, Christian, do we show appreciation for the spiritual nourishment we receive from the smallest reflection?

Standing in front of a pool of water, blending in the narrow creek bed, is a deer. The beast of the land kneels down to face its own reflection, lapping and satisfying its thirst.

Oh, Christian, do we show appreciation for the spiritual nourishment as we kneel and receive from a bigger reflection?

Soaring above a pond of water, resting between the hilly or rocky banks, is an hawk. The fowl of the land and water swoops down to face its own reflection satisfying its hunger.

Oh, Christian, do we show appreciation for the spiritual nourishment as we share our reflection in gathering places?

CHAPTER 9

Human Nature

The wolf also shall dwell with the lamb, and the leopard shall lie down with the kid, and the calf and the young lion and the fatling together, and a little child shall lead them.

Isaiah 10:6

illustration by Susan Laspagnoletta

CHAPTER 10

Revealing Lights

The revelation of Jesus Christ, which God gave unto him, to show unto his servants things which must shortly come to pass; and he sent and signified it by his angel unto his servant John.

Revelation 1:1

The last book of the Holy Bible was written by St. John the Divine.

He wrote specifically to seven churches of Asia. What did he reveal to these churches? What lessons, instructions, guidelines would these churches be given to show what is to come? How do these revelations compare to the lessons we learn from nature?

Jesus is revealed as the Alpha and Omega; the beginning and the end. Each life; whether physical or spiritual is affected by Jesus' teaching lessons to follow from birth; the beginning. This may be our physical birth as well as the birth of an idea, the birth of a church, or the birth of a nation. Nature portrays many forms of birth, the new shoot of a plant, an human infant, a newborn creature, or a new plot of land.

The births of seven churches of Asia are introduced by John as resembling candlesticks. Sources of light that could be hidden by darkness need to have a source of power just as we witness in nature.

The source of power for the Church of Ephesus would be love to shine the light of labour. God's sun shines as strong as His Son lights the way for His labourers.

The source of power for the Church of Smyrna would be light to shine the light of tribulation. God's lightning shines as strong as His Son prepares the way for His followers.

The source of power for the Church of Pergamos would be faithfulness to shine the light of true doctrine. God's creation continues as strong as His Son's reliable lessons for His students.

The source of power for the Church of Thyatira would be teachings to shine the light of charity. God's people share as openly as His Son's following of the Ten Commandments.

The source of power for the Church of Sardis would be perfection to shine the light of work. God's people follow the same Golden Rule as His Son's glowing resume!

The source of power for the Church of Philadelphia would be receiving the Holy Spirit to shine the light of an open door. God's people can receive the same Holiness as His Son's example in feeding the 5,000!

The source of power for the Church of Laodicea would be deep warmth surrounding the lives of those impacted by their ministry. God's people can take in the same deep warmth of the Trinity as His Son preached in the Upper Room.

Today the source of power for our churches could be powerful probe lights, laser beams, to shine the light for the 21st Century. God's people can continue to take in the penetrating light or the soft-glowing light of God's good news to be shared by His Son as He is quoted from The Holy Bible (the Alpha and the Omega; the beginning and the end) lessons that are revealed by light as bright as candlesticks!

CHAPTER 11

Pleasant Music

And the Lord God took man and put him into the garden of Eden to dress and keep it."

Genesis 2:15

Moses writes a descriptive account of God's creation of the Garden of Eden. While reading this account one receives a visual picture of nature and it is pleasant not only to the eyes, but also to the ear! The Garden of Eden is not silent but has music; any aesthetically pleasing or harmonious sound or combination of sounds (according to Webster's Dictionary")

Can't you hear the music of the whistling wind, clapping of thunder, slapping of the waves, dripping of the drops, rustling of the leaves, buzzing of insects, hissing of reptiles, murmuring of beasts and humans.

Moses even gives account (Genesis 4: 21) of how Cain's descendants handled the harp and organ as they raised cattle and lived in tents. The fowl of the air were probably imitated and the beast of the field. The main kind of music shared in the majesty of God the great Creator was recorded in Moses' book of Exodus 15: 1,2; the Lord being his strength and song.

I believe that God is my strength and gave me a song, another testimony of His majesty in my life:

Master of the Universe

You are the master of the universe
You have formed us with your hand
just as the earth and moon revolve around the sun
we need Jesus Your Son.

You are the master of the universe
You have formed us with your hand
just as the plants need the rain and the sun
we need Jesus Your Son.

You are the master of the universe
You have formed us with your hand
just as the early rising of the sun
we greet Jesus Your Son.

Words and song written in Oswego, N.Y.
Caregiver and Substitute Teacher 1990's

CHAPTER 12

Night Owls

But the cormorant and the bittern shall possess it; the owl also and the raven shall dwell in it.

Isaiah 34:11

The Prophet Isaiah is warning the people of the Lord's vengeance and the year of recompences for the controversy of Zion.

The four birds mentioned in today's scripture lived in Zion.

First we learn from the cormorant (water bird).
The cormorant was often identified as greedy with its hooked bill.
As children we were taught to share and not be greedy.
Oh Christian, do you learn from the comorant?
We are encouraged to possess what we are given while sharing the blessings!

Then we learn from the bittern (resonant crier);
The bittern was often identified as a bellower!
As children we were reminded how yelling and bellowing had its place!
Oh Christian, do you learn from the bittern?
We are encouraged to possess what we are taught while sharing knowledge!

Then we learn from the owl (nocturnal);
The owl was often not seen in the daytime; living in the dark!
As children we were seldom up past 8:30 hopefully resting in the dark!
Oh Christian, do you learn from the owl?
We are encouraged to dwell in the light from the darkness of sin!

Finally we learn from the raven (robber);
The rave was often stealing the food of other birds!
As children we were taught to ask for more food if hungry!
Oh, Christian, do you learn from the raven?
We are encouraged to dwell in salvation from spiritual hunger!

CHAPTER 13

Natural Resources

For the earth bringeth forth fruit of herself, first the blade, then the ear, after that the full corn in the ear.

Mark 4:28

illustration by Susan LaSpagnoletta

CHAPTER 14

Mustard

Another parable put He forth unto them saying, The kingdom of heaven is like to a grain of mustard seed, which a man took, and sowed in his field: which indeed is the least of all seeds: but when it is grown, it is the greatest among herbs, and becometh a tree, so that the birds of the air come and lodge in the branches thereof.
Matthew 13: 31, 32

When I notice the mustard plants along the roadside and the fields, I remember my parents telling us how the mustard plant with its bright yellow blossoms was as popular as the buttercups, dandelions, tree-foil, sunflowers, and the golden-rods in sharing their provisions for the fowl of the air.

When I researched the mustard plant I learned that the mustard plant is an annual plant with very small seeds and grows to a considerable size especially in Palestine. Here in New York, the size is not comparable to a tree but just tall enough to blend in the grass of the field.

Birds lodge or simply light in the branches of the sturdy mustard plant.

The seeds gathered by humans are crushed and powdered into today's yellow condiment! Their oily seeds were used to create a gaseous blistering agent during warfare; the volatile mustard gas.

Thus, a grain of mustard seed is comparable to the kingdom of heaven.

It's greatness and valuable resource for God's earthly creatures are also attributes along with brightness, color, and sturdiness.

Oh, Christian, the natural bright color of yellow; from the tiniest mustard seed, the flowers of the buttercup, the dandelion, and the sunflower and the beams of the sun are visual reminders of our dependence on God's Son!

CHAPTER 15

Limbs

I am the vine, ye are the branches: He that abideth in me, and I in him, the same bringeth forth much fruit; for without me ye can do nothing.

John 15:5

Jesus was giving a farewell sermon to His disciples which included answering questions asked by His followers:

Thomas asked Jesus if He knew the way!

(John 14:5)

Jesus knew the disciples could relate to the illustrations of the vine and the branches. Thomas realized that there could be no doubts or hindrances when following Jesus and while preaching of total dependence on his Lord Jesus Christ!

Philip requested that the Lord show them the Father

(John 14:8).

Jesus knew the disciples depended upon visual cues the vine and the branches. Phillip realized that there had to be total dependence on the leading of his Lord Jesus Christ!

Judas (not Iscariot) asked his Lord how He would manifest Himself to the world?

(John 14:22)

Jesus knew the disciples were designated preachers of the gospel (good news), and depended upon Him, His energy (as the vine) to bring forth fruit (as His branches).

Limbs from trees are preparing to bear fruit and some are being pruned (a natural process for trees) prior to this natural process.

Oh, earthly friends that may have had surgery to remove a limb, due to health reasons, do you recall how the rest of your body became stronger from rehabilitation and therapy?

Oh, earthly friends that may have experienced an ice storm or another type of natural cause that created havoc to trees of all sizes and how this could be called God's natural pruning?

Oh, Christian friends, a natural part of salvation and holiness is pruning from God so we can experinece saving grace and healthy spirituality in our daily lives from the only true Saviour Jesus Christ.

CHAPTER 16

First Bottle of Water

And Abraham rose up early in the morning, and took bread, and a bottle of water, and gave it to Hagar, and putting it on her shoulder, and the child, and sent her away: and she departed, and wandered in the wilderness of Bersheba.

Hagar was called a bondswoman. She and the son she bore for Sarah and Abraham were given provisions and sent away. Included in the provisions was a bottle of water. The water was depleted while wandering in the wilderness of Be-er-sheba. There was the searching for a well with pure drinking water available. Meanwhile, dehydration could easily set in especially within the child. Surely Hagar does not want to witness or have her son die a slow agonizing death from dehydration!
Her frantic searching finally comes to an end when God provides!

Hagar and her son would be in awe of the modern world of the ways of provision for water; from water bottles as big as a humans to storage tanks!
Yet, there is the existence of underground springs and wells providing the basic needs of God's creatures.

As a child, I livied on a farm in Pultney, New York (near Prattsburgh). I recall the discovery of an underground well, the experience of prining the porch pump, and boiling water to prepare for good tasting drinking water.

As a student and young adult living in a rural community, I recall the first time drinking from a water fountain (most of it running down my chin and neck)!

I also recall the first taste of water water machines placed in offices and public places.

As an adult I have knowledge of the advantages of drinking pure water to prevent dehydration and to this day have acquired a liking for water at most of my meals. Water quenches my thirst! Water is often given the label by farmers as; Adam's ale!

Oh, Christian, do you allow the spiritual, pure water that only God provides to hydrate, supply, nourish, and keep your soul cleansed?

Oh, Christian do you allow God to provide and fill you to the brim?

CHAPTER 17

Back to Nature

Thus saith the Lord, which giveth the sun for a light by day, and the ordinances of the moon and of the stars for a light by night, which divideth the sea when the waves thereof roar; The Lord of hosts is his name.

Jeremiah 31:35

illustration by Susan LaSpagnoletta

CHAPTER 18

Time By The Sun

Preach the word, be instant in season, out of season, reprove, rebuke, exhort with all longsuffering and doctrine.

II Timothy 4:2

The Apostle Paul was writing to a young leader; Timothy. Time was important to both Paul and Timothy. Paul had seen many more sunrises and sunsets than Timothy. Paul's ministry would be steady and as reliable as a sun-dial.

As a child and sibling of two sisters and two brothers of the 1950's, I recall the importance of relying on the sun-dial or the position of the sun in the sky. Especially in the late afternoon, the chores were waiting and supper would follow as we noticed the nearing of the sun to the horizon or our home-made sundial in the woods indicating late afternoon hours!

As an adult I recall the leaders in my life that had seen more sunsets and how they taught me to be a leader, minister in The Salvation Army and to preach. One such friend I preached to in New York City in 1975 and today 2013 we continue to correspond about our continuing to preach while being led by the words of the Apostle Paul: In and out of season (wherever, however, whenever) preach the word!

If Apostle Paul and Timothy were to be preaching in 2013 they would be able to read, hear, text, search the web, and even tape the words preached by powerful speakers of our time. One such is a preacher of holiness; Samuel Logan Brengle who preached way back in the 1880's.

His sermon of holiness included his love for all of God's creatures and sanctification; holiness of the purest form."

Preaching does not always come from behind a pulpit, or by reading excerpts from commentaries or references from other preachers. Watch for the opportunity in and out of season; with the rising and setting of the sun, and most importantly in times of reproof, rebuke and sharing experiences.

CHAPTER 19

Palms

And a very great multitude spread their garments in the way; others cut down branches from the trees, and strawed them in the way.

Matthew 21: 8

How many Palm Sundays have you celebrated? How many times have you been reminded of Jesus' entry into Jerusalem as palm branches are spread along the path of garments where Jesus would be riding a lowly and young animal (perhaps a colt or donkey)?

As a child, I took a turn riding a donkey on Palm Sunday! I took my turn at Sunday School at the Methodist Church in Prattsburg, New York. Luckily the donkey had a blanket to cushion the bouncing we were receiving as we joined in singing and waving palms. I remember singing; Tell Me The Stories of Jesus and trying hard daily to give Christ a place of honor in my life.!

As an adult I not only learned how palms were laid out for Christ, but the importance of the sincere proclaiming of Hosannas as I raised my palms toward heaven in honor of the risen Christ; the King of Kings; The Lord of Lords! Every Palm Sunday I am reminded of the young child at The Salvation Army Long Point Camp in Penn Yan, N.Y. who led me through the path of salvation with the raising of her palms toward the hand-made cross which stretched toward heaven. She spread her joy of the Lord along the paths of Long Point Camp and others joined and picked up where she started! I am one of those joiners and follow the path of our triumphant Lord and King Jesus Christ!

CHAPTER 20

Early Bird Special

And he sent forth a raven, which went forth to and fro, until the waters were dried up from off the earth. Also he sent forth a dove from him to see if the waters were abated from off the face of the ground.

Genesis 8: 7, 8

Moses gives account of Noah's opening the window of the ark of animals and family after forty days of floods. Genesis 8:6

The raven and the dove are the earliest birds to be mentioned by name and given a misson; to rise from sleep or arrive prior to specified time of a special occasion.

The raven is the first to be sent out by Noah flying to and fro. Moses does not record the fate of the raven. We can imagine that the raven with its large size and wing span traveled far and beyond; not returning to the ark perhaps due to discovering an environment more appealing than the ark!

The dove is sent out by Noah to fly to and fro and brought back evidence that the waters were abated by carrying in its beak an olive branch. We can imagine that the dove being of smaller size returned to the ark perhaps due to finding a twig to start a home in the ark!

The lessons of the raven and the dove are parallel with our lives when we are sent to and fro. Will we take advantage of the specials? Will we be early birds upon arriving at the point of salvation and in receiving holiness?

CHAPTER 21

Nature Director

Now learn a parable of the fig tree: When her branch is yet tender, and putteth forth leaves, ye know the summer is near.

Mark 13:28

illustration by Susan LaSpagnoletta

CHAPTER 22

Planted Trees

The Spirit of the Lord is upon me; because the Lord hath annointed me; to proclaim, to comfort, to appoint unto them, to give unto them that they might be called trees of righteousness, the planting of the Lord, that He might be glorified."

Isaiah 61: 1-3

Isaiah was a prohet who testified that he was appointed by God to preach the good tidings. He had scrolls to carrry to his appointment. He did not have the Holy Bible as we know today. Trees and plants were used and still are today. He had tablets to carry as he proclaimed. He did not have the cassette or cd as we use today. Stones and rocks were used and still are today.

As a child I remember the attempts to write on the bark of white birch, the slate of stone found in the creek, and the smooth surface of tree stumps. I even learned how to use berry juice and sap from plants to leave messages!

As an adult I continue to write with the use of tablets of paper, chalkboards, dry eraser boards, typewriters, and computers to leave messages. My attempts at writing are my proclamations toward my God!

CHAPTER 23

Weekly Weeder

And that which fell among thorns are they, which when they have heard, go forth, and are choked with cares and riches and pleasures of this life, and bring no fruit to perfection.

Luke 8:14

Jesus teaches to his followers in this parable a lesson of preaching and showing the glad tidings of the kingdom of God.

Luke 8:1

As I write this devotional I think of the dandelion (I call the King of Weeds)!

You have to be a weekly weeder to keep up with the royal pain of this plant!

Oh yes, we are fascinated by its white blowing seeds, its bright yellow flower, its tangling roots, and the long dominating stem. This delectable and edible plant can also choke the flower of the field and the seeds can travel a long distance as if claiming all the land around!

I think of how we all start out our day being influenced by the seeds of family life, and the impact of breathing in, breathing out, feelings, attitudes, words, actions, wisdom, emotions, expectations and even the sharing of the glad tidings of God's kingdom. We are weekly weeders of God!

If Isaiah had access to today's technology I believe his techniques may be different but not his message: May the Lord be glorified !

CHAPTER 24

Metamorphosis

And be not conformed to this world: but be ye transformed by the renewing of your mind, that ye may prove what is that good, and acceptable, and perfect will of God.

Romans 12:2

The Apostle Paul wrote an epistle to the Romans and introduced himself as a servant of Jesus Christ who offers grace for daily apostleship

(Romans 5).

The twelfth chapter of the epistle from Paul to the Romans contains a vivid description of metamorphosis; a transformation or marked change aappearance (Webster's Dictionary). I immediately picture a butterfly! I have seen butterflies in their different stages of metamorphosis and see them as a perfect object lesson. I imagine the Apostle Paul would agree! What a beautiful way to compare our lives when allowing God's conformity!

As a child I recognized the physical appearance of myself more than anything else. Would I always be one of the shortest in the class? When would my acne clear? Will I wear the dress that I made in Home Making class to church?

The outward appearance dominated my thinking!

As an adult I began to notice inner transformation which resulted from my total surrender to salvation and holiness. This metamorphosis in a Christian's life is total surrender to the Trinity; Father God, His Son Jesus Christ, and His Intercessor The Holy Spirit.

CHAPTER 25

Nurturing Nature

When I consider thy heavens, the work of thy fingers, the moon and the stars, which thou hast ordained; what is man, that thou art mindful of him?

Psalm 8: 3 & 4

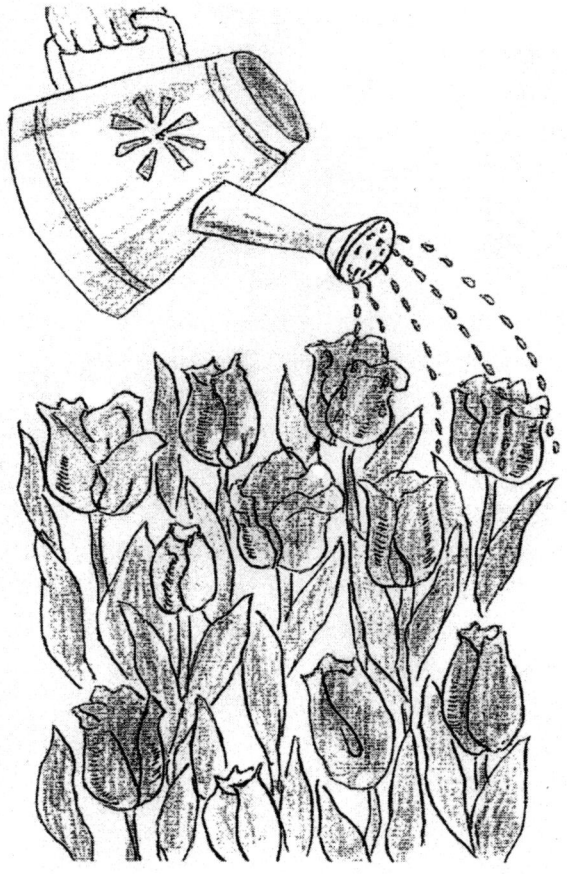

illustration by Susan LaSpagnoletta

CHAPTER 26

Quiescence

Judas (not Iscariot) saith unto him, Lord, how is it that thou wilt manifest thyself unto us, and not unto the world?

John 15:4

Here in New York during the month of March the temperature can change drastically from the 60's to a chilling 30's! The flowers and trees must be at times confused! I know we humans are baffled as we watch the starting of blooms and buds!

In researching about the dormant season of seeds (called quiescence), I learned that a plant slows in response to environmental cues and ceases to grow. If conditions change such as an early thaw new growth my show. Also during this dormant season there is a second stage of rest which is controlled from within the seed.

Dear Christian, our Lord has chosen to be with His Father; God. We do not see Him visually as did His followers. We only physically see our Lord through the art work of painters; illustrators. Jesus can be pictured by images we create in our minds by words that describe Him! Take for instance His words in a parable that states that He is the vine and we are the branches. What an image of a fruitful vineyard!

What an image we collect when Jesus states that He is the Great Shepherd and we are the sheep of His pasture! Natural circumstances illustrate the stages of quiescence for us and we can apply what we learn from nature to our way of life as Christians. How patient are you?

CHAPTER 27

Rehabilitation

And Zaccheus stood and said unto the Lord; Behold Lord, the half of my goods I give to the poor; and if I have taken anything from any man by false accusation, I restore him fourfold.

Luke 19: 8

Saint Luke (one of the four gospel authors) wrote to Theopholis, giving instructions and an account of Jesus Christ's life and ministry.

Luke 1: 3 & 4

After Luke (the physician) gave vivid accounts of Jesus' royal birth, childhood, and early start in ministering, he recalls the conversations of Jesus with one of his followers; Zaccheus (tax collector!). His curiosity of Jesus; so admired by others caught his attention! He climbed a tree to get a better view (secretive viewing)!

Luke describes how Jesus caught sight of Zaccheus and invites him to come and dine with Him! Oh, Jesus knew rehabilitation was starting for Zaccheus as he confessed to Lord Jesus what needed to be done first; restitution (paying back) and rehabilitation, (gaining forgiveness for squandering).

If Saint Luke was a doctor of the 21st century, his techniques may vary but not his message. Rehabilitation comes first by personal awareness, acceptance and allowing oneself to receive therapy for restoring oneself to a good condition.

As a child in the 1950's I recognized the family and school for ideal preparation for adulthood which often included rehabilitation and restoring the good in life.
Jesus, my Saviour was already getting involved in a subtle way!

As an adult in the 1980's I required rehabilitation and restoring of my emotional and physical condition with the help of my families (biological and extended) and restoring the good in life. Jesus, my Lord continued to be involved in a clear way!

As an adult in 2013 I am reminded of recent rehabilitation and restoration of my physical, social, emotional and spiritual condition with the help of the extended family I live with and the caring team to restore the good in life. Jesus, my guide continues to be involved in an adventurous way!

CHAPTER 28

Circulation

And he said unto them, go ye into all the world and preach the gospel to every creature.

Mark 6:15

Jesus gives a command to His apostles just after a memorable resurrection!

He urges them to circulate and share the message of salvation through their Christ!

Circulation according to Webster's Dictionary is the movement in a circuit as a result of action such as distribution. Circulation is a natural process for humans, plants, creatures, rivers, and even newspapers!

As a child I remember studying about the biological circulation the most fascinating to me being nature's hidden circulatory process that becomes evident in the changing of the seasons! Just as fascinating is any living thing's circulatory system that also becomes evident in the changing of the age!

As an young adult I witnessed medical advances towards enhancing the circulatory system for my Grandma Seabury as she became a recipient in the 1960's for a heart pace-maker.

As a college student I recognized the power of circulation of water during a major flood in the Finger Lakes area of New York State. I was working at The Salvation Army Long Point Camp and we staff circulated the grounds by leaping from one picnic table to another just for one day as we were promptly given assignments to assist flood disaster victims. I was assigned to Hornell NY and the aid provided included the circulation of sharing the message of salvation just as the apostles did for their Saviour Christ Jesus. The process of circulation may have been different but the message remained the same in the 1970's.

As an adult I recognized the power of circulation of knowledge during a power outage in Oswego, NY (an April ice storm). The circulation of electricity was literally stopped for a week! Circulating to family and friends at that time was limited. Circulation of heat was from the oven (shared with a dog and bird that I was pet-sitting)! Circulation or distribution of food worked out okay (thanks to the improved storage bins of the 1990's)! There was even the circulation of Christian material in that small kitchen area as I shared my morning devotions with a dog and a bird!

As a fourth time author I recognize the power of circulation of the Good News of Salvation for all through Christ our Saviour. As I type on the computer here in a shared home with Phyllis, Barbara and Corkie on Ritchey Blvd. Crystal Beach (Gorham, NY) in 2013, I share my limited process of writing (typing). The computer reveals the same results as any other circulatory system. There is movement, distribution and clogs along the way! I believe God has created pace makers in our professions to assist us along the way! His team members; Jesus and the Holy Spirit work together for a natural, smooth, flow for the moving along of the message of salvation to all the world.

CHAPTER 29

Natural Beauty

And out of the ground made the Lord God to grow every tree that is pleasant to the sight, and good for food; the tree of life also in the midst of the garden, and the tree of knowledge of good and evil.

Genesis 2: 9

illustration by Susan LaSpagnoletta

CHAPTER 30

Lingering Lilacs and Lilies

Consider the lilies how they grow, they toil not, they spin not; and yet I say unto you that Solomon in all his glory was not arrayed like one of these.

Luke 12:27

Lilies have a lingering aroma and beauty. Some may find its odor powerful!

In Jesus' time lilies as well as roses, aloe, rue, dill and spikenard were described as plants that taught us lessons! I add to this list the powerful lilac of today!

Let us visit the house of Simon the leper in the city of Bethany. Jesus sat and ate meat. There came a woman with an alabaster box of ointment of spike and poured it on Jesus' head (Mark 14:3). Oh the disturbance that day to some of Jesus' followers was due to what they stated was a waste of precious oil while we know prophecy was being fullfilled.

Let me revisit the house of my childhood years in Prattsburg, New York. I would take in the powerful aroma of the lilac bushes. There came a day when those lilac bushes almost came to their end due to a run-away fire created by my mother on a real windy day. Oh the disturbance that day to us five Appelt children was real and our powerful aromatic lilac bushes would be overpowered by the singed odor from burnt wood from the back wall of our outhouse! All this would be due to a runaway ash from the burning drum located far away usually!

Let me revisit inside our country house on Stone Road. Mother and Dad allowed us children to gather flowers from the fields of the farm. There came a day when that gathering came to an end due to the choosing of bringing into the house milkweed pods. Oh the disturbance those plants created as the dry air would create a lingering cloud of fluff throughout the house. Oh the natural beauty of that plant was shortlived!

Let me revisit the lives of my parents in Prattsburg since the 1950's and from their second home in Portal, Arizona. My parents while raising a family of five children left a lingering beauty, aroma, example, and powerful lives for us.
This year (2013) on May 31st would be their sixty fifth wedding anniversary.
Precious memories how they linger!

Let me hold on to those precious memories and those my Saviour Jesus Christ allows us to revist daily! My Lord and Savious rose for you and me while lingering on the cross. Oh the disturbance that day on Calvary would be overpowered by the lingering aroma of the empty clothes found in the sepulchre on that first Easter. Consider the many anniversaries with its precious memories that linger for us in the Easter Lilies of the twenty first century!

Let others visit our homes, enter our lives and recognize their same Saviour Jesus Christ allowing us to consider the powerful example of the aromatic and significant influence of the lilies brought and savored!

CHAPTER 31

Blossom Like A Rose

The wilderness and the solitary place shall be glad for them, and the desert shall rejoice, and blossom like a rose.

Isaiah 35:1

Blossomed roses are gorgeous and so colorful! Some people may not be able to get beyond their thorny stems though!

In the Bible Dictionary the word rose indicates possibly a crocus or the oleander; the rose of Sharon. We read in the Holy Bible of how the writer of Song of Solomon states that he is the rose of Sharon.

The blossom of a rose is quite a sight! In Isaiah's and King Solomon's time the rose of Jericho was a dried weed, which opened when in water. In Jesus' time the word rose was used to describe the miracle at Easter. Just as the blossom of the rose leaves such beauty and majesty amidst its thorny and dried up stems, Jesus has left such beauty and majesty amidst the thorny and dried up crown placed upon his head. He arose amidst the solitary places to allow us to take in the beauty and majesty of salvation and holiness!

Do I allow my life to blossom like a rose; no matter my physical being and my immediate enviroment? I would like to think that I have blossomed not only in age every year on my birthday; June 23rd but that I represent the flower of the month of June; the rose daily. The birthdays have flown by and so have the years since I became a Christian in my twenties. I look forward to many more years of blossoming for my Saviour and Lord Jesus Christ.

CHAPTER 32

Act Naturally

For, lo, he that formeth the mountains, and created the wind, and declareth unto men what is his thought, that maketh the morning darkness, and treadeth upon the high places of the earth, the Lord, the God of hosts is his name.

Amos 4:13

llustration by Susan LaSpagnoletta

CHAPTER 33

The Ark of Gopher

Make thee an ark of gopher wood the length shall be three hundred cubits the breadth of it fifty cubits and the height of it thirty cubits.

Genesis 6: 14,15

Moses wrote of an ark of gopher wood that God instructed Noah to construct.

The length would be 450 feet, the breadth 75 feet and the height 45 feet. God was allowing Noah to prepare a place of safety for the arrival of the flooding of the earth. The drawing of this first ark is shown in the Bible Dictionary and is an impressive size! God's blueprint for Noah to follow included the necessary precautionary measures for this major flooding of the entire earth. We know Noah followed with precision and was allowed to bring God's creatures on the finished Ark. God's blueprint for Noah included salvation for his family.

I recognize that God's blueprint for each of our lives includes the building of our lives in preparation for Jesus' return and for our reaching our heavenly home. We may have survived flooded homes, businesses, fields of harvest and even our lives. God's blueprints for each of us are individualized and involves our careful following of them.

I wonder how Noah prepared the actual construction of the arkof gopher wood? He had to take in consideration the construction of three stories; room enough for the animals that would come in twos, his family and provisions. He must have carefully listened to his God for directions. He sure did not have a manual or any kind of reference book to follow! Noah's example of trusting God's wisdom is worth following. God must have chosen Noah for this feat for other reasons to; Noah's ability to construct, perhaps a man with what we call today common sense or being a natural at building; construction.

I recognize that God's construction of our lives is solely in preparation for being with Him; our Heavenly Father. While He and His Trinity Team (Jesus and the Holy Ghost) have prepared a place for us, we are being allowed to construct our lives where we have been chosen to be born, chosen to do, chosen to join, or even chosen to share our abilities. Constructing of a building may not come as a natural process for me, but I have witnessed and been a part of the Appelt Construction; the farm's milkhouse in Prattsburg,

New York and the solar, stone home in Portal, Arizona. The witnessing of these constructions completed in the 1960's and 1990's perspectively have been lessons for me and a reminder of how God is allowing us to choose how to daily construct our lives in preparation for our heavenly home. Let us daily be reminded that God needs to be the master builder and we have His blueprint to follow.

CHAPTER 34

The Ark of Bulrushes

And when she could no longer hide him she took for him an ark of bulrushes put the child therein; and she laid it in the flags by the river banks; was found by the Pharoah's daughter, nursed by a maid and the child grew and became her son and named him Moses.

Exodus 2: 3 and 10

Moses wrote of his own fate in the second book he is known to have authored!

He recalls how the daughter of Levi had been hiding Moses already for three months. Now she was relocating him once again and would be found by some dignitary! The ark of bulrushes constructed by the daughter of Levi is depicted in the Bible Dictionary as a very humble dwelling; secluded but yet attainable. All this transpired in preparation for the construction of a future leader's life.

I wonder how Moses felt about his beginnings; that he recorded for us to read? I know that he recognized eventually that God's planning; constructing is perfectly planned. I recognize the control God needs to have on my daily life too!

I recognize how God needs to be in control of our daily beginnings and endings as we age; as we mature; as we allow His perfect timing.

CHAPTER 35

From Arks to Ships

And Jonah rose up to flee unto Tarshish from the presence of the Lord, and went down to Joppa; and he found a ship going to Tarshish, so he paid the fare thereof, and went down into it, to go with them unto Tarshish from the presence of the Lord.

Jonah 1: 3

God allows Jonah to go into hiding. We could say that Jonah is the first recorded stow-a-way! But, he did pay to go as he tried to flee from the Lord and the uncomfortable situation! The ship was sailing to Tarshish and would be sturdy enough to survive the tossing waves of the sea. I ponder a moment to picture the construction of the first ship for the sea in comparison to Noah's Ark built for the flooded earth.

We are familiar with Jonah's predicament as he is cast into the sea and how he prayed to his God from the belly of the fish. We could say that Jonah not only paid to go on the ship, but he also paid for his decisions and actions.

God allows us to make choices on our earthly journey to heaven. Today we have all kinds of transportation means for our journeys; destinations. We also have choices involving the payment plans for our travels. We need to keep in mind that we will pay for our individual decisions and actions.

God is always prepared to lead us even when we flee from Him.

CHAPTER 36

Cargo

Now when we had discovered Cyprus, we left it on the left hand, and sailed into Syria, and landed at Tyre, for there the ship was to unlade her burden, and finding disciples, we tarried there seven days; who said to Paul through the Spirit, that he should not go up to Jerusalem.

Acts 21: 3, 4

Saint Luke writes about the Apostle Paul and how as a missionary he spread the good news of Jesus Christ's salvation and resurrection for each one of us. We could say Paul was on several cruise ships which also served as cargo ships. In Paul's case (according to Luke the doctor and log keeper on board) the goal was to arrive safely at Tyre. It was recognized as one of the best harbors of the Eastern Mediterranean Sea according to the Bible Dictionary.

The ship would unload its cargo. The crew and passengers would fulfill their itinerary; their mission. Often this involved meetings, conferences or even a rally.

Not all that was planned came about, however! Paul was given advice; a warning not to go up to Jerusalem. Paul as an Apostle was not always welcomed and followers of his mission were neither.

Perhaps some of you readers have been on cruise ships heading for a destination which involved planning that may have been changed. The crew may have been given advice; a warning not to go to the actual planned destination.

You may have been a member of the crew or one of the passengers finding out you were not encouraged to stick to the original itinerary due to hints of what we call today breaches of security. Diversion may have been set up.

What about the diversion of the cargo? Perhaps some of you readers have experienced the task of finding your baggage relocated; hopefully waiting for you at your final destination!

Dear readers of NATURE'S LESSONS, we have arrived at the end of this book's journey. My mission for this book as with HORIZONS, PONDERING OUR HORIZONS, & PONDERING PEARLS OF WISDOM has been based on sharing, testifying of the lessons I have learned on my personal journey as a Christian.

Oh, there have been diversions as cargo(or burdens) have been relocated (or lifted). It is how we take and learn from nature the lessons of life in the form of advice and or warnings that prepares us for future cruises in life!

I look forward to meeting with you on my next cruise which I have already set up an itinerary! My next book is already in the planning stages and already has a title: PRACTICAL MEMORIES. See you soon! God's blessings!

Sincerely, Patricia L. Appelt
& Susan A. LaSpagnoletta

CPSIA information can be obtained at www.ICGtesting.com
Printed in the USA
BVOW05s1817131014

370606BV00001BA/68/P